Growing a Sustainable Soul

Growing a Sustainable Soul

Bob Flanagan

ST. MARK'S PRESS

www.stmarkspress.net

WICHITA, KANSAS

St. Mark's Press
8021 W 21st St N
Wichita, KS 67205-1743

Phone:	1-800-365-0439
Email:	stmarkspress@gmail.com
For orders and information:	stmarkspress.net

Cover Design: Diana Hubin
Interior Design: J. Ted Blakley

ISBN 10: 0-9839899-1-5
ISBN 13: 978-0-9839899-1-2

For Caity

whose love for good soil
and farming sustains me.

Contents

Introduction

Semi-Millennial Reconfigurations

The twenty-first century is a time of dramatic change. The economies of the world are transforming. Geopolitical forces are unsteady. Social movements rise and fall in quick succession. Rapid advances in technology make life easier but create new vulnerabilities to our personal privacy. Such dramatic times of change, while unsettling to live through, are not new to human history nor are their impact on social institutions like the Church.

History demonstrates that the Church has always undergone dramatic changes. As Phyllis Tickle notes in her book, *The Great Emergence: How Christianity Is Changing and Why*, every five hundred years the Church undergoes a "tumultuous reconfiguration" or "re-formation," in which the Christian faith "births" a new sense of self. These "semi-millennial eruptions" ultimately change the Church for the better.

Five hundred years ago Martin Luther nailed his 95 theses on to the Castle Church door in Wittenberg—the sixteenth-century version of posting on Facebook. Other notable reformers of the time included John Calvin and Richard Hooker. Yet of equal importance during the same period was the rise of Spanish mysticism, as expressed best in the works of Teresa of Avila and John of the Cross. Their religious writings were not only important to those who first read them, but they have been a gift to Church ever since, read by countless Christians in each succeeding generation.

Five hundred years before Luther and company, the Great Schism occurred. Because of deep theological divisions and differences in local expressions of worship, the Church split, creating the Eastern Orthodox church and Western Christian church. In spite of the split, the Church did not fall apart but rather just expressed itself differently. For instance, Pope Gregory VII ended marriage within the clergy, solving two major issues that had hindered appropriate expression of priestly duties. Most importantly, the church became a major unifying force and a stabilizing institution during a troubled time in Europe.

Pushing back another five hundred years, during a time when the Roman Empire transformed significantly, Christianity expanded throughout Europe. With the end of the formal structures of the Roman Empire, smaller kingdoms arose. Christianity grew within and through these new powers. Supporting the expansion were monasteries. Benedict of Nursia established monasteries in Italy and, significantly, wrote the Rule of St. Benedict. On the remote island of Skellig Michael, six miles off the coast of western Ireland, monks established beehive monastic cells, demonstrating the power of eremitical and ascetical life to the Irish people, who enthusiastically embraced Christianity during the sixth century. Monasticism helped stabilize Europe at a time great tumult.

Of course, five hundred years earlier a young, devout, Jewish woman gave birth to a boy named Jesus. Within one hundred years, a new monotheistic religion arose in a pagan-dominated world. The slow but steady decline of paganism commenced, and the world was forever changed.

Now, in the midst of the fourth semi-millennial reconfiguration of Christianity, we don't fully understand what the changes occurring are and how we will emerge from them. No doubt, the church will emerge different. No doubt, there has been and will be more discomfort for those living through it.

Yet, like the previous "re-formations," there are positive developments. Most notably has been the change in our relationship with the land. Industrialization of America led thousands of people to the city, forgoing a centuries-long relationship with the soil. We went from a country where most Americans were born on a farm to one where few are farm-raised. To cope with the dramatic population shift and labor loss, farm practices mechanized, and now, few people work in fields. Fewer people know what good soil is. Our food has become packaged and precooked. Our vegetables and fruits sit neatly in piles of uniform color and freshness, regardless of the time of year.

The Soul's Heartache

The effect of the lost contact is not just physical; it is spiritual, too. Our souls ache to connect to the land in healthy ways, to experience rich soil between our spiritual fingers. In order to satisfy this ache many people attempt purposeful interactions with the land. For many years, nature conservancies and local, state, and national parks have attempted to meet the need, but more recently many have turned their interests to food. Organic food sales have grown significantly. Community-supported agriculture programs—a method of purchasing food from local farms—have become more sophisticated and popular. They provide many with ways to connect with the land through eating better food.

Affirming this connection, the Bible tells of a people who lived in a land where the relationship with the soil, water, and earth infused their life. The land of the Israelites existed in an arid climate with diverse soil and topography, inconsistent rainfall interspersed with sudden and violent deluges, and occasional deep droughts. Yet, even with these challenges, the land provided. The Israelites called the land of Canaan a place flowing with milk and honey (Exodus 33:3). Biblical people lived close to the land and knew how to care for it. In return, the land sustained them.

Importantly, the Israelites expressed their linkage to the land in biblical writings. The Bible—an ancient library of divine revelations—includes the writings of the Hebrew Scriptures. These writings express the Israelites' relationship with God through their history. God continually drew near to the Israelites in order to guide them into righteousness. Often biblical writers found examples of God's righteousness revealed in the arid climate, diverse soil, and bountiful land.

Righteousness and Sustainability
The word "righteousness" feels old and unfamiliar. We may not know or use this term frequently. However, the Hebrew Scriptures mentions it more than five hundred times and the New Testament more than 225 times. A simple translation is acting in a morally right manner.

A better way for us to understand righteousness, especially in its relationship with sustainability, is through the sound wave concept of resonance that is found in music. When someone plucks a string on an instrument such as a guitar, it creates a sound wave. As the wave travels outward and reaches a similarly tuned string on different guitar, for instance, the second string will vibrate. Physicists calls this action forced vibrational motion.

Carmelite scholar Dr. Keith Egan first introduced me to the concept of resonance. He uses resonance as a trope in preparation for reading and understanding mystical writings, like that of Teresa of Avila and John of the Cross.

Resonance, however, is far greater than a part of physics or a preparatory tool. Resonance is all around us. The soul is like a twelve-string guitar. Soul strings resonate at a certain frequencies. Additionally, the soul senses the frequencies produced by the soul waves around us. When one soul interacts with other, both souls resonate, and certain soul strings play. Sometimes in harmony and sometimes not. Furthermore, creation resonates. Each created thing and nature as a whole resonates. God resonates, too.

Righteousness occurs when the soul resonates with others around it and with God. Righteousness doesn't stop there, however, the soul resonates with nature. Moreover, the soul, nature, and God may all resonate at once. A friend of mine told me of an experience he had recently—one you have may have had at some point as well—when he stood outside on a clear, cold winter's night. At the time, he was considering the third and fourth verses of Psalm 8: "When I look at your heavens, the work of your fingers, the moon and the stars that you have established; what are human beings that you are mindful of them, mortals that you care for them?" He suddenly felt humbled.

What happened to him? When he looked up at the night sky, his soul strummed a note. As that soul wave left him, creation began to resonate. It played the exact same note. Moreover, God played that note, too. My friend entered into a mystical space. Such space is rich with holiness, yet it is also a space of righteousness. When his soul resonated with creation and God, he felt humbled. His feeling is a natural result of resonance. He felt righteousness, a moral reaction to resonating with nature and God.

Righteousness is the natural expression that emerges from resonate interactions with creation and God. Dr. Ellen Davis aptly defines it: "Righteousness means living in humble, carefull, and godly relationship with the soil on which the life of every one of us wholly depends." To live rightly, therefore, is not simply to live morally well with our neighbors, but it is to live morally well with the soil and the environment—God's creation.

Sustainability fits snugly with righteousness. Yet, unlike righteousness, sustainability is a new word. We toss it around like a feather in the air. It still is malleable, changing with its usage by the culture. So it is best to give several definitions in order to discern a more complete understanding of sustainability.

> In ecology, where the concept was first given force, sustainability refers to how biological systems endure and remain diverse and productive. Long-lived and healthy wetlands and forests are examples of sustainable biological systems.
>
> WIKIPEDIA

> The "greatest good for the greatest number" applies to the [number of] people within the womb of time, compared to which those now alive form but an insignificant fraction. Our duty to the whole, including the unborn generations, bids us to restrain an unprincipled present-day minority from wasting the heritage of these unborn generations."
>
> THEODORE ROOSEVELT, 1916

> A sustainable United States will have a growing economy that provides equitable opportunities for satisfying livelihoods and a safe, healthy, high quality of life for current and future generations. Our nation will protect its environment, its natural resource base, and the functions and viability of natural systems on which all life depends.
>
> THE PRESIDENT'S COUNCIL ON
> SUSTAINABLE DEVELOPMENT

What we see in these secular definitions is that sustainability has a moral component to it. Living morally well with biological systems has a positive effect not just on our neighbors but also the future majority to which Theodore Roosevelt referred. We need natural resources to prosper. Thus, sustainability and righteousness, values so deeply held by the Israelites, are crucial and close partners.

How we treat the world, its environment and resources, connects us to God. In fact, we are three interdependent partners: Humans, Creation, and God. The partnership functions best when it resonates. It will only do so when morally recognize how we connect to everything around us and act in supportive ways to everything that is.

CHAPTER ONE

A Sustainable Soul

The breath of God is only one of the divine gifts
that make us living souls; the other is the dust.

WENDELL BERRY

Still Waters

He leads me beside still waters;
he restores my soul.

PSALM 23:2B–3A

I'm drawn to water, especially the still waters of a cold, deep lake. It's special, holy, and sacred. The undisturbed reflection of the world shining back at me feeds my soul. Given how many of us live within just miles of the oceans, besides lakes, or near rivers, I'm not the only one who feels this way. All of us are drawn to water, especially still waters.

Why? It is only in the reflection of still water that we can see ourselves as we are. It is in calmness that we can self-reflect. And only in still water can we see what is underneath the surface. So much of philosophy and modern psychology asks for us to see ourselves, self-reflecting and searching for what lies underneath the surface of our actions. In this process we discover who we are, we discover why we're here, and we are sustained.

At the heart of the sustainability is the call of God. For thousands of years most of humanity lived directly connected to the earth. But now, living in modern countries, so few of us connect with the land to sustain our lives. Rather we connect with creation by going to the grocery store or the farmer's market, or looking longingly at the water as we commute to and from work.

God, however, calls out to our souls to return to the soil and to return to still waters. The lingering longing to care for the land, air, and water is more than single-mindedness, coming out of a sense of naturalistic do-goodness. No. In part, God calls us to return to the very things that sustain our bodies and souls. Still waters, for one.

❧ Action

On the next calm day, go to the ocean, a river, or a lake. Sit still for twenty minutes. Ask yourself: "How is God restoring my soul?"

_____

_____

_____

_____

_____

_____

_____

_____

_____

_____

_____

_____

_____

_____

_____

_____

_____

_____

_____

Fresh Cut Grass

May he be like rain that falls on the mown grass,
like showers that water the earth.

PSALM 72:6

The psalmist calls upon God to bless the great Israelite king Solomon. He wishes that Solomon's rule may be as nourishing and gentle for the people of Israel as rain feeding freshly cut grass. The author desires only the best for this new leader. He's hopeful and expectant that Solomon will bring greatness to the land and the Israelites.

How I long to be blessed in such a way. Who among us wouldn't want to have leaders who could lead in such a way as if we were nourished by a gentle hand? But life isn't that way. Our work is hard. Our bosses are demanding. We search for extra time and struggle to find peace.

Yet maybe life doesn't have to be this way. What if we approached what we do in a nourishing and gentle way? That is at the heart of a sustainable soul. Imagine you're planting seeds. Would you treat them gently and nourish them with life-giving and life-sustaining water and sun? Of course you would.

Moreover, we want our own souls to be treated the same way. We want to feel nourished in all we do. We want the gentle hand of our divine creator nourishing us. Sustainability is more than simple actions that help the environment. It is a way of living and a way of being. Nourishment and gentleness.

ℰ Reflection

Name five ways to feed your soul.

_____

_____

_____

_____

_____

_____

_____

_____

_____

_____

_____

_____

_____

_____

_____

_____

_____

_____

_____

_____

_____

_____

_____

_____

_____

_____

_____

_____

_____

_____

Parched Places

The LORD will guide you continually,
  and satisfy your needs in parched places,
  and make your bones strong;
and you shall be like a watered garden,
  like a spring of water,
  whose waters never fail.

ISAIAH 58:11

I once followed a mountain river all the way back to its source. Given the force of the water a mile below, I expected to find a lake. I scrambled over boulders and hopped from rock to rock. Even a few hundred yards from the source, I expected at least a pond. I stepped over the watercourse, leaving footprints in the soft moss-covered ground. As the stream narrowed, it still ran quickly. Then suddenly, it stopped. I backtracked. The bubbling sound guided me to the water's source. I stooped. Water flowed from an unseen reservoir. The river started as a spring. High up the mountain, the stream came to life.

What is the source of life? What causes the seed to break open and fight upward through cold, damp soil? How is it that cells divide and multiply? Where does the water come from? The cause of all is our almighty, wondrous, and beloved God. As Isaiah writes, God continually guides, satisfies our needs, and makes us physically strong, like a spring-fed garden.

Yet there are days and seasons of our lives when we are parched. There seems to be no stream bubbling up from our soul. These times are necessary parts of life. They cause us to pause and search within and without for help and hope. As God guides us through these times, we are able to grow, not as a flower on a warm spring day, but as roots searching for spring-fed water, deep underground. Through it all, we are sustained by God.

℘ **Reflection**

How does God sustain the environment through difficult time, through periods of drought or flood? What happens to the environment after these times? How has God sustained you when your soul has dwelt in parched places and times of drought?

_____

_____

_____

_____

_____

_____

_____

_____

_____

_____

_____

_____

_____

_____

_____

_____

_____

_____

_____

_____

_____

Lightning

Now as Paul was going along and approaching Damascus,
suddenly a light from heaven flashed around him.

THE ACTS OF THE APOSTLES 9:3

On a clear, cool, summer's evening in the Adirondack Mountains, my daughter and I snuggled under a blanket on a lounge chair staring skyward. We admired the night sky. I pointed to constellations and named them. She asked questions. I answered them with the best of my lay astronomical knowledge. She spied satellites cruising across the arc of the nighttime dome. Suddenly, the sky lit up. Flashes from heaven. Stars disappeared. The sky went from black to white to black again. We anticipated the thunder, but it never came. Flash followed flash. The celestial bodies disappeared and reappeared over and over. A distant storm electrified the night, but the folds of mountains and valleys muted the thunder.

The abrupt flashes of light captivated my curiosity, like the smell of warm pot of stew that draws me to the kitchen on a cold afternoon. What is the cause of the flashes? Where is the storm? Why is there no sound of thunder? Flashes of light transfix you and me, and that is what Paul must have felt on the road to Damascus. Divine light shrouded him, causing him to stop, making him fall off his horse. It is the light that changed him. The light of God made him a Christian. Without the light, Paul may have ignored the voice of God, but the flash made him stop to listen.

The power of light, not just sunlight but also lightning, disrupts, captivates, and transfixes us. Because of it we stop. We anticipate the thunder, but the thunder is not what's important.

The light is. The light brings out the truth. The light is what changes our souls. The light shows us the way. God may speak to us often in many ways, but we must pray for the divine flash that will cause us to hear him.

ಹ **Reflection**

Remember the last lightning storm you witnessed. Ask yourself: How did I feel? Why? What did your soul say in those moments?

_____

_____

_____

_____

_____

_____

_____

_____

_____

_____

_____

_____

_____

_____

_____

_____

_____

_____

_____

_____

Flowers

The flowers appear on the earth; the time of singing has come, and the voice of the turtle-dove is heard in our land.

SONG OF SOLOMON 2:12

Could the beauty of a flower be so great that it causes the flower to tremble in awe of God's handiwork? What if the flower said to God, "I'm too beautiful; it's too much for me; it's more than I can take; it will kill me"? You may laugh at the thought, but why? What's more powerful: a dozen roses or just one?

New love is never more deeply defined than by the singular beauty of one red rose. It's lure. It's luster. It's careful fold upon fold, in perfect red. Its sensuality is heightened by the prick of a thorn. Care must be taken when handling such exquisiteness. The rose is a vessel of God's overflowing creativity and love.

You and I are like flowers. We can become vessels of divine creativity and love. When we seek God, asking to be signs of his love and splendor, we become the overflowing wonderment of God's handiwork. Of course, we're created by God, but I'm suggesting more than that. If we open our heart to God, we feel a beauty that is too beautiful to keep inside us. We must share it with others or else that beauty overwhelms us. We are the rose in the hand of a young lover.

ℰ Action

Bring cut flowers into your home. Gaze at them in awesome wonder. Consider how you are like what you see.

_____

_____

_____

Storm

Deep calls to deep at the thunder of your cataracts;
all your waves and your billows have gone over me.

PSALM 42:7

When I think of the ocean's edge, my memory releases images of tranquil waves curling on top of the sandy shore, rhythmically matching the beat of my heart. I enjoy the feeling that floods over me. There is, however, another image, one I suppress.

Recently, I watched a video shot by a friend of the shoreline near his home. It was dotted with tremendous rock formations and strewn with boulders. Waves thundered and rolled over and around the rock and boulder obstacles, agitating against a bit of sand before smashing upon tall cliffs. Plumes of mist surged skyward. Chaotically and unceasingly a cacophony of "shurr" filled the air.

Imagine for a moment swimming in my memory—a happy thought, right? Now consider floundering in the other water. When I do, my throat immediately tightens because I know I would be tossed about, thinking only about my next breath. Regardless of my swimming skills, I wouldn't last long. Neither would you.

If I were someone who believed in only black and white, in only good and bad days, and no shades in between, these images would speak of my life. Although I don't subscribe to such simplicity of life, I appreciate the stark difference presented by a tranquil water image and a chaotic one. As the psalmist writes, there are times when the thunder of the life's cataracts wash over all of us, creating days filled with labored breaths. Life is simply too much. I've had these days: the bills are too many and money is scarce; people ask too much of me at once; no one understands how tough my life is; I'm lost.

I don't like those days. But they are only days, and they pass. We don't swim forever in the turbulent waters of the rocky shore. Like anyone, I have a distaste for those days, yet it is within them I cry out for the God of power, the God capable of creating this world. When I watch the waters pound against rock, I am struck at just how great God is. Although I love the pastoral shepherd who leads me beside still waters, I need the mighty God whose purposes have shaped the firm shores of life's troubles.

ᨑ Reflection

Think of your toughest and most trying days.
Was God there? If so, where and how? If not, why?

_____

_____

_____

_____

_____

_____

_____

_____

_____

_____

_____

_____

_____

_____

_____

_____

Darkness

Wild waves of the sea, casting up the foam of their own shame; wandering stars, for whom the deepest darkness has been reserved forever.

JUDE 1:13

What is darkness, if not the absence of light? Darkness is more than that. It is the siren call of the chaos in the world. Its dreadful silence reminds us that nature controls us more than we it.

Consider the storms of recent years: As trees mingle with wires and wild waves cast about the shorelines dotted with homes, we relearn darkness. Human nature blinds us to chaos. We forget lessons from years gone by and blithely ignore the chaotic realm of wild waves; thus darkness emerges from the chaos. Our souls long for waterside dwelling, and our minds trick us into the tolerance of inconvenience. We build on sand and allow branches to become enmeshed in electrical wires. We even dismiss sick and withered trees tottering near our homes. Then chaos returns. We dwell in darkness until the power returns and homes are rebuilt, logs stacked, and branches chipped into mulch.

Is this the sustainable existence we seek? No. A day without power is an inconvenience. After a week most of us struggle, and when it's longer—anguish. Homes filled with water or washed away disturb us deeply. House split by massive trees darken our spirits. Authorities scold us, like petulant children, into shame, convincing us we've earned this deep darkness. I bristle at the accusation.

Sustainability is about adaptability, not mere tolerance of chaos. What is it to be human, if not to learn and grow? Chaos looms forever, just beyond the fringe of the cast light. Nonetheless, our fate is not to be forever buffeted by wild waves and languish in the deep darkness. Our soul calls out to mold our circumstances into a better, more sustainable approach wherein the chaos is tamed by our intellects, like clever children solving a puzzle with ease.

ℰↃ **Action**

Donate to a charity that helps people suffering from storm damage. Better yet, within the next year, volunteer and help rebuild homes in a storm-damaged area. Consider what you will learn about darkness.

Deer

As a deer longs for flowing streams,
so my soul longs for you, O God.

PSALM 42:1

Not long ago, I returned home and spied a doe and a buck in a grassy field close by. She was alert, flicking her ears up as I quietly settled my foot on the car brake. With four pointed antlers curving skyward and spreading far beyond his shoulders, the buck slowly raised his head. Watching me with cautious curiosity, the pair looked wholesome and hale.

I imagine these deer softly padding the woods in search of water. They avoid the bogs across the road. With their soft, muddy surroundings, the deer wouldn't venture in there for fear of becoming stuck and vulnerable. Nor would they want to drink from the lake down the hill. Waves beat a steady slosh against the shoreline so to cover the approach of a predator. The deer prefer the soft bubbling of a stream surrounded by small trees and brush. Its movement of water ensures freshness. The quiet engenders security. The protected surroundings allow the deer to relax, rest, and find peace.

My soul also longs for a place to relax, rest, and be at peace. Where do I find that place? When I sit next to the orange glow of an early winter's fire. As I stroll along the lakeside path surrounded by tall trees, standing stoically as if on watch. In the fading light of a hot summer sunset. After a sudden spring rain, smelling the pungent aroma of earth bursting to life. Creation sustains my soul. In its multitude of splendor, my soul links to the God.

❧ Action

Get outside today and feel connected to God. Write about it.

My Body, God's Temple

Do you not know that you are God's temple
and that God's Spirit dwells in you?

1 CORINTHIANS 3:16

How differently would we act if we truly bought into Paul's words? Would you make different choices when purchasing food? Would you eat and drink differently?

There are times when I try to treat myself as God's temple—or at least think about it. I pick out fresh fruit, instead of prepackaged snacks. I drink water instead of soda. I get enough sleep. For a time, I treat my body like God's temple, but then life gets in the way.

Bad days make it difficult for me to be temple-esque. On those days, I reach for the cookies, or a scoop or two of ice cream, instead of an apple. I guzzle caffeine-ladened cola rather than filtered water. I scrimp on sleep. Tough days are temptation-filled, not temple-dwelling.

I wonder if I do so poorly out of spite: "Hey, God, why did you make the world so tough?" Life is difficult. And there is part of me that shakes my fist at God because of it. But is it really?

Many of us, though not all of us, live pain-free days. I'm not talking about the occasional cold or headache or arthritis. I mean chronic, debilitating pain. Thankfully, most of us glide through life. I know I fail to appreciate such carefreeness all too often. I think it is normal. It's normal to lose perspective. It's common for us to forget the beauty that surrounds us and especially the beauty within. If we agree that we're divinely created, we must house the Spirit of God. Thus, no matter the day, the circumstance, or conditions, we are called to treat ourselves as holy, good, and valuable. What a difference that viewpoint makes.

ଊ Assessment

Think about the times when you treated yourself poorly.
When were they? What caused them?
How did you move on from them, if you have?

_____

_____

_____

_____

_____

_____

_____

_____

_____

_____

_____

_____

_____

_____

_____

_____

_____

_____

_____

_____

Fire

Then Moses said,
"I must turn aside and look at this great sight,
and see why the bush is not burned up."

EXODUS 3:3

There are few things more alluring than a fire. The time of year makes no difference to me. I am mesmerized by a late summer evening's camp fire or fire pit, just as I am entranced by a midwinter's fire in a fireplace. The licks of light dancing above the logs captivate my eyes. The hot, red embers hypnotize me. Flames soothe my soul.

Fire's importance in our lives cannot be understated. Making it became our first technological advancement. Controlling it was one of our first skills. It was one of our first defenses from the elements and predators. It was one of our first weapons. Fire was also our first luxury. It was the thing that demonstrated how different we were from any other creature on earth. For most of humanity's existence, with the exception of these modern times, everyone knew how to make and use fire, and understood how it worked. So when Moses saw the burning bush he instantly knew it was different.

The burning bush was more than a common fire; its purpose was far greater. Enmeshed in the storyline of the burning bush is how God uses fire to create a fire in Moses' soul. Like the bush, his soul-fire doesn't burn up. Because of his encounter with the most alluring of fires, Moses leads his people out of exile, through the wilderness, and into freedom. While we might not stumble upon a burning bush, kindling a fire in our soul is no less important for us. It will be the fire within that draws others to see how we care for the world and by it how we may inspire others.

ℰ Assessment

Ask yourself: "How passionate am I about sustainability? What part of it gives my soul fire? How can I grow my soul's fire to care for the earth more?"

_____

_____

_____

_____

_____

_____

_____

_____

_____

_____

_____

_____

_____

_____

_____

_____

_____

_____

_____

_____

_____

_____

_____

CHAPTER TWO

The Power of God

*The sun was mounting up with those stars that were with
it when God's love first set those lovely things in motion.*

DANTE ALIGHIERI
INFERNO I:39–40

The Hawk

Is it by your wisdom that the hawk soars,
and spreads its wings towards the south?

JOB 39:26

When I was in my twenties, the hawk returned to southern Connecticut. I first noticed it by its lonely shrill that pierced the silent, humid haze of summer. "Peeshurrre. Peeshurrre." I could hear it before I could see it. Shielding my eyes from the white sky, I looked above the thick canopy of dark green maple and oak leaves. I heard but still didn't see it.

Its call was so different from familiar sounds of summer. The chirp and chatter of chickadees and sparrows filled low bushes and trees. The cacophony of cicadas and crickets deafened the night. Squirrels barked at each other as they raced in spirals up trees. The hawk's cry, however, was majestic and solitary. It spoke of a knowingness and confidence that were mysterious, like the power of an atom or moonlight illuminating a snow-covered field.

As I finally glimpsed the hawk soaring far above, I marveled at its power to harness the air and effortlessly glide in long, lazy circles. And yet the hawk does not fly purposelessly. From high above it searched for prey, unseen by me. From where does this hawk come? By whose power does it command the sky? Not ours. No. Its power comes from God.

&O **Action**

Take a walk and observe nature. Seek ways to see God's power
sustaining the world. Ask yourself: "In what ways does God sustain the world? How am I connected to the world? How does
the world touch my soul?"

_____

_____

_____

_____

_____

_____

_____

_____

_____

_____

_____

_____

_____

_____

_____

_____

_____

_____

_____

_____

_____

Overflowing Joy

The pastures of the wilderness overflow,
the hills gird themselves with joy.

PSALM 65:12

Each summer my family and I leave the coastal lands of New England and head south. We travel down the Shenandoah Valley, up and over the Appalachian Mountains that divide Tennessee and North Carolina to the Blue Ridge Mountains. As we venture from the urban areas of the Northeast, I always marvel at the bounty of the land. What riches the land produces! From the farmlands of Pennsylvania and Virginia to heights of the Smokies, we live in a country overflowing with green.

My heart and soul sing with the joy of the wilderness. How is it that our world produces such riches? Where does this constant and continuous fruit of the land come from? Oh, you and I can speak of the science of the land. Yes, we understand the basic ecology of our environment. We know that seeds emerge from the soil. Plants and trees grow in the summer's heat and sun and feed on the nutrients of the soil, rain, and sun. But the deeper question is, "What is the cause of it all?"

When I pause to consider the spark that causes the "wilderness to overflow" and the hills to "gird themselves with joy," I am simply overwhelmed with awe and wonder. My soul sings, "How great Thou art!" Does yours?

ଅ **Reflection**

What in God's creation brings you joy?
Where do you see the wilderness overflow?

_____

_____

_____

_____

_____

_____

_____

_____

_____

_____

_____

_____

_____

_____

_____

_____

_____

_____

_____

_____

_____

_____

_____

_____

_____

_____

True Power

> *Jesus said to them, "For truly I tell you, if you have faith the size of a mustard seed, you will say to this mountain, 'Move from here to there,' and it will move; and nothing will be impossible for you."*

MATTHEW 17:20

In human terms, power comes from authority and the ability to control others. It is also found in the capacity of one person to withhold things, like another person's autonomy and freedom. It can also be seen as being able to command others and to make people do things.

God uses power in a completely different way. Consider the mustard seed. Jesus notes that the power of this tiny seed is great because, from a tiny seed, it will grow into an enormous plant. Unlike human power, which is used to control, limit, and restrict as much as it allows for freedom, God's power is all about growth and renewal. A tiny seed, unseen unless diligently sought after, grows into a plant multiple times bigger than the seed. This power is not to be ignored, though we often do. We take it for granted. It is so robust and encompassing, yet, day in and day out, we fail to give it its due consideration.

We talk about footprints—carbon footprints, for one. How do we compare even seven billion footprints to a single ridge of God's fingerprint? We can't.

We have two responses to God's power. One is awe-filled respect. The other is to align our use of power more and more with God's ways of using power. We cannot love God without respecting creation. We cannot be truly devoted to God and use power more to limit and restrict than to allow for growth.

ଚ Awareness

There are three types of power: the power to restrict, the power to allow, and the power of growth and renewal. How do you use these types of power in your life?

_____

_____

_____

_____

_____

_____

_____

_____

_____

_____

_____

_____

_____

_____

_____

_____

_____

_____

_____

_____

_____

_____

_____

_____

_____

_____

_____

_____

_____

_____

Chaos or Order

And after the earthquake a fire, but the LORD was not
in the fire; and after the fire a sound of sheer silence.

1 KINGS 19:12

God is not a god of chaos. Elijah's world is in disarray; he is on
the run and is desperate to understand why everything is falling
apart. He needs to make sense of the chaos consuming his
world. So he spends forty days and forty nights in the wilderness. An angel comes to him and directs him to Mount Horeb,
the same place where Moses met God. There he encounters
God, whose purposes create order.

But before he does, Elijah stands on the precipice and ex-
periences the full chaos of nature. First a wind so strong that it
splits mountains descends upon him. Next come an earthquake
and then a fire. God is not, however, within each of these. God
comes after these terrible, soul-rending events. God is in the
sheer silence. God is not in the chaos, but in the ordered things.

To me, there is great comfort knowing that God is about
order. At times our world seems out of control, that there is no
order. When droughts dry up crops, storms tear apart coastlines,
and fires rage feasting on acre after acre, the world thrashes
about as if it's having a grand mal seizure. Yet after the drought
comes rain, after the storm comes calm, and after the fire comes
new life, some of which only happens after a great fire or ex-
treme heat, like jack pine seeds. The cones of this serotinous
pine only open after a fire reaches a certain temperature. Then
it releases its seeds. And importantly, the Kirtland's Warbler, a
beautiful, little song bird, needs young jack pines to live. Order
out of chaos.

The power of God may seem empty compared to some of nature's greatest events of destruction and chaos, but in the silence after the storm, new life emerges. Light defeats darkness. Life outlasts death. Order emerges from chaos.

ॐ Reflection

Where in your life is there chaos? Where is there order? How do the two work together? Where do they battle each other?

_____

_____

_____

_____

_____

_____

_____

_____

_____

_____

_____

_____

_____

_____

_____

_____

_____

_____

_____

The Rainbow's Promise

God said, "This is the sign of the covenant that I make between
me and you and every living creature that is with you, for all future
generations: I have set my bow in the clouds, and it shall be a sign
of the covenant between me and the earth."

GENESIS 9:12–13

I awoke one morning to my wife's call. She urged me to hurry
to her. When I arrived she excitedly directed my attention
across the field in front of our home. A rainbow arched up
from just beyond the tree line. It was a sign that the day would
be beautiful, and indeed it was.

I don't know about you, but there are days when I become
overwhelmed by the magnitude of the earth's environmental
challenges. When I hear reports about how hot recent summers
have been in comparison to ones measured in the past, I feel
drained. When I learn that the polar icecap in the Arctic has
receded significantly over the past ten years, I want to toss up
my hands and give up. How do my recycling efforts help with
such big problems? Really, what positive effect does my driving
a hybrid make to the weather? Does turning off an extra light in
my house really help stop the icecap from receding? My little
actions seem like a child trying to hush the wind.

Then there is the rainbow. When I saw the colorful arc
spreading high across the sky, I remembered God's promise.
God's covenant with Noah means there is a greater force at
hand, working to keep things right. And with that in mind, I am
reassured that my efforts, puny as they may seem, are worth-

while and valuable. They are simply my response of thanksgiving to the God almighty, who promised to sustain our world, even when we can't.

ꙮ **Action**

What new step can you take to help the environment, which at the same time gives thanks to God?

_____

_____

_____

_____

_____

_____

_____

_____

_____

_____

_____

_____

_____

_____

_____

_____

_____

_____

_____

_____

The Foundation of the Earth

God said,
"Where were you when I laid the foundation of the earth?
Tell me, if you have understanding.
Who determined its measurements—surely you know!
Or who stretched the line upon it?"

JOB 38:4–5

I once saw a video showing the Hubble Space Telescope's view of a deep space field. At first, there was nothing but black space, which was the reason the scientists pointed the telescope in that direction. Then images of hundreds of galaxies came into focus. As the telescope peered deeper into the field, and, by doing so, traveled back in time, clearly formed galaxies passed from view and only blobs of light remained. Deeper into the space field and only a few nascent galaxies stayed in frame. Then, suddenly nothing. There were no blobs of light, just darkness. The beginning of the universe.

Where were we when God laid the foundations of the earth? We weren't. God created the foundations of the earth at the Big Bang, the conception of the universe. We are made from stardust, the leftovers from exploding and dying stars. Time needed to pass, eons come and go, before life's onset. Only after billions of years could the universe sustain complex life, like us, those who can consider the origins of existence. The universe is no child, but we are.

Where were we when God laid the foundations of the earth? We were simply a potentiality of a divine idea, like seeds that grow only after fire ravages a forest. Therefore God must love us greatly for him to be so patient, waiting billions of years, before we could come into existence. A patient and loving God. That sounds nice. Doesn't it?

ℰↃ **Action**
Praise God. Praise God for all that is good in your life. No matter how much trouble or what the challenge you may be experiencing, praise God.

CHAPTER THREE

The Right Use
of Resources

*And care for the earth expresses the fullness and vastness
of the God whom we love and serve.*

STEVEN BOUMA-PREDIGER

Lost Sheep

Jesus said, "Suppose one of you has a hundred sheep and loses one of them. Does he not leave the ninety-nine in the open country and go after the lost sheep until he finds it?"

LUKE 15:4

On occasion I bless sheep. A farmer friend of mine contacts me after her new flock is born and invites me over. I walk among the sheep, praying and sprinkling them with holy water. Well, that's the idea. The trouble is sheep are skittish and cautious around strangers. Fortunately, they love to eat. So, with my friend's help and coaxing with food, the flock gathers close enough for me to do my work.

What is remarkable is that the farmer knows her sheep. She knows them just as a friend knows the face of a best friend. To me, they all look the same. To her, each one is valued and valuable. She readily identifies them, and if I miss one or two, she tells me. She also knows if one is missing.

What makes sustainability so important is that every creature is valued and valuable. God has created everything and everyone, and thus, naturally, he values all creatures and all creation. All is valuable, even if we don't know it. From the tiniest bug, to the largest of trees, and the greatest of whales: all have a purpose and a value to God and creation. This makes sense, right?

As actors in this world, we have the power, bestowed on us by God, to value and find value in all of creation. We are called by God to seek out the lost—persons and creatures—and in doing so we honor creation, ourselves, and God.

ཡ **Reflection**

What is the least valued creature in creation? What is its value? How can you keep it from being lost? What is the most valued creature and why?

_____

_____

_____

_____

_____

_____

_____

_____

_____

_____

_____

_____

_____

_____

_____

_____

_____

_____

_____

_____

_____

_____

_____

_____

_____

_____

Mist

I have swept away your transgressions like a cloud,
and your sins like mist;
return to me,
for I have redeemed you."

ISAIAH 44:22

Mist is fine water drops, not falling from the sky as much as hanging in the air It waits for us to enter into it. Unlike many types of rain, mist is more soaking. Without realizing it, a few minutes in mist can leave us soaked through.

I love waterfalls. Niagara Falls is, of course, one of the greatest. And it generates plumes of mist, like clouds billowing up from a cauldron of boiling water. But the power of the falls, with their noise and churning water, overwhelms the mist. A smaller waterfall, like Montmorency outside Quebec City, is a better mist-producing waterfall. The mist is just fine enough and full enough to soak someone without him or her knowing it. In just a matter of a minute or two, the mist drenches anyone who ventures too close.

Imagine now, our sinfulness and abuse of natural resources being swept from us like mist. Without exception, all of us have taken advantage of the splendor of the natural world. We buy. We consume. We throw out waste. Each step impacts the world. If we want to be a sustainable soul, what do we do then? Can we live in such a way that we create no abusive or sinful impact on the world we live in? Probably not.

A sustainable soul is not one that creates no footprint on the sands of the world; rather it is one that creates the least harmful imprint possible. We do so by recognizing our negative tendencies, seeking forgiveness from God, and recommitting ourselves to better living. Each time we do, we learn how to use the gift of creation in a more just and righteous way.

❧ Action

Travel to a waterfall nearby or watch a video of one. Think about its power. Observe its force. See the mist. Imagine what it feels like to be soaked by the mist and how to dry off. Consider how that soaking is like your use of resources and how drying off is like God's forgiveness.

Water

A garden fountain, a well of living water,
and flowing streams from Lebanon.

SONG OF SOLOMON 4:15

The most valuable resource of the twenty-first century is living water. More than any source of energy, living water will be central to the flourishing of humanity between now and the turn of the century. I'm not saying there will be no water on earth within 100 years, as if we would become a second Mars, dusty, arid, and void of habitation. When I speak of living water, I'm referring to water that gives life.

Not long ago, archeologists found a religious purification site on the banks of the Jordan River in Israel. It was a large, walled, bath-like structure with stairs leading down to where a pool of water would have been. Unlike the spa-baths of today, however, this site had a hole at the bottom of two walls. Their purpose was to allow water to flow, in one side and out the other. The movement of water gives it life.

Think about it. Stagnant water is still. Water that is not in motion festers with organisms that make it undrinkable. It's not life giving. It smells. It is discolored. It is unclean and tastes bitter and acrid. Life-giving water is the opposite. It doesn't smell; it's clear and clean; and it tastes wonderful.

Many of us use life-giving water as if it's limitless. We turn faucets and let them run. Why not, the water is always there. Yet it is not. Most water, in the world today, is undrinkable, and we'll find that our habitual overuse of clean water will make living water scarce and a source of deep conflict, posing difficult questions about whose water is it.

ℰↄ **Reflection**

Whose water is living water? What role does God play in such water? As children of God, if living water becomes rare, how best should we distribute it and use it?

_____

_____

_____

_____

_____

_____

_____

_____

_____

_____

_____

_____

_____

_____

_____

_____

_____

_____

_____

_____

_____

_____

_____

_____

Subdue the Earth

God blessed them, and God said to them, "Be fruitful and mul-
tiply, and fill the earth and subdue it; and have dominion over the
fish of the sea and over the birds of the air and over every living
thing that moves upon the earth."

GENESIS 1:28

Subdue and have dominion. These are powerful words of in-
struction that God leaves with us. They require responsibility.
They demand just use and wisdom. They call us to find the best
way to rule. So how have we done with the power bestowed on
us? Have we been responsible? No easy answer there. Like a
parent, giving small doses of freedom, God has left us this earth.
What kind of children have we been with our responsibility?

Preschoolers? Maybe. Like children set loose in the kitchen
for a few minutes, there have been times when we've pulled out
all the pots and pans from the cabinet and dumped the flour on
the floor. Uh-oh. Our answer to the mess: "I don't know!"

Grade-schoolers? Like children holding up pictures of their
houses and families, including pets, we've looked with pride on
our attempts to control our environmental messes. We've
beamed with self-satisfaction at our ability to cultivate the land
into breath-taking amounts of produce.

Teenagers? Many times we've charged ahead with the bra-
zen confidence of teenagers, insisting our care and use of natural resources are justifiable, only to discover we've destroyed
more than we've cared.

Adults? Maybe we're getting closer to that image. It seems
we've finally opened our eyes to the limits of our ability to subdue

and control. We've begun to see the true effectiveness of a light touch.

Dominion requires the gentleness of a caretaker, not the pride of a rambunctious teen. Subduing the earth doesn't mean destroying it. Our rule of the earth requires the eye of an artist, the wisdom of an ancient elder, the passion of a poet, and the love of a child.

৪০ Action

Do something right now. Not later today, but right now, to help the environment. Take a step toward a more sustainable earth. Think. Act.

_____

_____

_____

_____

_____

_____

_____

_____

_____

_____

_____

_____

_____

_____

_____

_____

_____

Gleaning

When you reap the harvest of your land, you shall not reap to the very edges of your field, or gather the gleanings of your harvest; you shall leave them for the poor and for the alien: I am the Lord your God.

LEVITICUS 23:22

Gleaning is a term that has lost its significance. When we entered the industrial age and gave up our close connections to the land, we left villages and hamlets for the city. In doing so, the land became foreign to us, but more importantly, we lost touch with our moral compact to each other, especially the poor.

I've longed to reestablish my portion of the compact. Recently, I've changed what I bring into Boston with me. I pause before heading out to ensure I have the trio of care warrants, namely, a piece of fruit, socks, and a dollar. They're not much, but in part, that's the point. A gleaning is the leftovers of the harvest. God commands, not suggests, that the ancient Israelites to leave a small amount of the harvest in the fields, nothing substantial, but it was enough to sustain the poor of the village or hamlet. Without it they would starve. God creates a moral compact between farmers and the poor.

Our work with the earth, our consumption of the goodness and fruits of our labors, and God's continued sustaining of the land cannot be completed without understanding the moral significance of our work. What we do matters not just to ourselves, but to the poor. The sun, rain, land, and seeds are gifts bestowed to us by God. God simply asks in return for us to work the land, enjoy the bounty, and leave some for the poor and hungry. The right use of resources demands a moral responsibility.

ℬ **Action**

Check with your local food pantry and determine what they regularly need. Then make a permanent list of "giveaway" goods that you bring to the store with you each week. Twice a month or more drop off the goods you collected. Or check with your store manager to see if the store has a food collection program and leave your donations there.

_____

_____

_____

_____

_____

_____

_____

_____

_____

_____

_____

_____

_____

_____

_____

_____

_____

_____

_____

_____

The Right Use of Resources

Jesus said, "From everyone who has been given much, much will be demanded; and from the one who has been entrusted with much, much more will be asked."

LUKE 12:48

Every one of us has been given much, nothing more so than our food supply. In thinking about how we get the food we eat, I'm convinced that there isn't a single lazy farmer in America. It's not possible, because a lazy farmer is not a farmer for long. Farming is tough work, but it is also immensely rewarding. We entrust farmers with growing our food, and, even greater, we entrust farmers with our lives.

The transporters of our food and the merchants who sell us our food have our trust, too. They have been given a great responsibility, to get our food to us quickly and carefully. We don't want spoiled food. We don't want food that will kill us.

We have a responsibility as well. Our responsibility is to demand much from those who have been given much, our food growers, transporters, and merchants. To some extent we've given away our responsibility to our government when we entrust them with the quality of our food, especially from our large food growers. But today's sustainability movement illustrates that not all of us are comfortable with the relinquishment of such responsibility. And one solution to the discomfort of some has been small farms and the farmers who work these small, local farms.

Small farmers feel the responsibility of what has been given to them, because they meet those who eat their food. There is an honor that comes with a farm stand. The interaction that takes place is not simply financial. It is a transaction of trust: Look what I've done with what I've been given. It is good. I've used my resources well. The farm stand interaction is sacred. What's more, that sacredness should push us to demand such interactions of trust from all famers, even from the large agri-businesses.

∞ Action

Go to a local farm and introduce yourself. Be curious and learn as much as you can about what and why the farmers grow what they do. If you live in an urban area, find a farmer's market and do the same. Write a plan to bring local food into your diet.

CHAPTER FOUR

Jesus the Gardener

Biblical support for Jesus the master carpenter is minimal and not definitive. Instead, the Gospel evidence points in another direction: Jesus the expert gardener.

The Gardener

Jesus said to her, "Woman, why are you weeping? For whom are you looking?" Supposing him to be the gardener, Mary said to him, "Sir, if you have carried him away, tell me where you have laid him, and I will take him away."

JOHN 20:15

It's pleasant to think of Jesus as a carpenter. He learns his craft from his father. I easily imagine him as an eager young boy, happily watching his father craft lumber into a home or furniture. Jesus follows his dad each morning as he sets off, tools in hand, to a home he's building. Maybe Joseph gives Jesus his own tools, when he's old enough. And Joseph begins to teach him how to properly hold the hammer, how to cut lumber with steady precision, and how to carefully work a chisel. This image strengthens the relationship between earthly father and son. It's nice to think this way, but it's not supported by the weight of scripture.

The Gospels show us another Jesus. This Jesus tells agrarian parables. He speaks about the land. He ties the coming kingdom of God to plants. Conventional thinking tells us he does this because that is what most Galileans would understand—as if they didn't live in houses built by a carpenter's skill. We need to call this thinking into question.

Scripture points us in another direction: Jesus the expert gardener. Over and over again, he teaches using creation as his example. From vineyards to seeds, Jesus ties his moral teachings to the land. So maybe, in the garden on Easter morning, Mary misidentifies Jesus because Jesus naturally, in his very core, is a gardener, one who draws from the land its full potential.

℘ **Reflection**

Read three or more parables of Jesus. Notice how he uses lessons from the land. Think of Jesus as a gardener. Ask yourself: "How does this change my image of Jesus?" Imagine Jesus working in a garden. See Jesus anew.

_____

_____

_____

_____

_____

_____

_____

_____

_____

_____

_____

_____

_____

_____

_____

_____

_____

_____

_____

Germination

Jesus also said, "This is what the kingdom of God is like. A man scatters seed on the ground. Night and day, whether he sleeps or gets up, the seed sprouts and grows, though he does not know how."

MARK 4:26–27

One day I was looking at the vine of peas growing in a bucket of dirt outside my front door. The plants were not much to behold, but it was the best I could do given the lack of an area to plant a vegetable garden. Nonetheless, those peas were hardy and determined. I wondered what made them grow. It's a thought I often have when looking at seeds. I'm perplexed and awed whenever I think about how seeds grow. Given the vicissitudes of the world, the growth of a tiny seed into a large, robust, food-producing plant is remarkable, even often miraculous. Things just grow.

While we have manipulated the process of germination and forced certain kinds of plants to grow to our liking, we don't control the process. As Jesus said, "Night and day…the seed sprouts and grows." We may understand the process of germination, pridefully thinking we grasp it completely, yet there still is mystery in it, like heat coming from somewhere beneath the darkened ashes of a fire. As in all of life, the necessary conditions must be met before life occurs. We know that these conditions include water and nutrients, but there is a bit more to germination. Something fundamental, imbedded in all living things, is required: the breath of God. Although you and I can't point at this divine wind, deep in our souls we understand truth of this necessity. Our wonderment at the germination of a seed is more than enough evidence to affirm its truth. When God breathes, seeds grow, and everything grows because of it, even you and me.

❧ Reflection

Read Jesus' parable from Mark 4 about how seeds grow. Contemplate the cause. Ask, "Where is God?"

_____

_____

_____

_____

_____

_____

_____

_____

_____

_____

_____

_____

_____

_____

_____

_____

_____

_____

_____

_____

_____

The Fig Tree

Then Jesus told this parable: "A man had a fig tree planted in his vineyard; and he came looking for fruit on it and found none."

LUKE 13:6

I once planted three hydrangeas in the front yard just after the last post of a split rail fence. They were young, small and bloomed the first season. They never bloomed again which was and still is a frustration. I babied those plants: fertilizing, watering, pruning, and protecting them. They grew quite large. Each season I got on my hands and knees and closely inspected each plant. Nothing but healthy leaves.

So what to do? Should I have pulled out the hydrangeas or kept holding onto hope that they might bloom? I often thought of the fig tree parable of Jesus when considering what to do with the bloomless plants. In the parable the man wanted to tear down the fig tree. His gardener said to wait just one more year and the man did. We never learn of what happened to the fig tree. Did it bear fruit or not? Was it torn out of the ground?

The parable is not about whether the tree bears fruit, is it? No, it's about what to do when a fruit tree is doesn't produce. And what's more, the parable asks a deeper question: what is the worth of a living thing? The gardener tells the man that he will give the tree extra attention during the next year. The gardener's response is central to the worth of the tree. He will care for the tree, and then the man can decide what to do once he sees the result of the gardener's care. We can't judge the value of creation unless we take time to care for it. For creation to provide us sustenance, we must tend to its needs by giving it extra care. We can't assume that creation will give us what we need if we don't tend to its needs. The parable points to the interconnectedness of us and creation. We are all its gardeners.

ℰ Action
Go to a market or gardening center and ask a clerk or manager what do they do with plants that do not bloom. Ask to buy one for a discount, then care for it. All the while, think of Jesus' story of the fig tree. Keep track of what happens as you care for it.

_____

_____

_____

_____

_____

_____

_____

_____

_____

_____

_____

_____

_____

_____

_____

_____

_____

_____

_____

_____

Wind and Sea

And Jesus said to them, "Why are you afraid, you of little faith?"
Then he got up and rebuked the winds and the sea; and there was
a dead calm.

MATTHEW 8:26

Every afternoon in the spring, I motor a launch around a large lake while coaching a rowing team. It's a pleasant way to spend an afternoon most days, but not all. There are days when I wished I had Jesus along to rebuke the wind and the waves. On those days, I am constantly adjusting my steering to stay next to boats I'm coaching. If I stop, the wind immediately pushes my bow one way or another. I do more steering than coaching.

How Jesus calmed the waters is a mystery. Matthew makes it sound so simple, so easy. I understand that Jesus is different, but there is a ho-hum to the whole event. He gets up and rebukes the elements. Not only that, but he chastise the disciples, too. As if they had his power. Do they? Do we?

I've never tried to rebuke the wind and waves. Why would I? Our environment is so vast and complex. Its systems belie a power we can't and will never fully understand. These systems are a mystery. Remember when someone described how a butterfly flaps its wings in China and there's a hurricane in the Atlantic. The complexity of how it all works, and I don't think for a second it's simply chaos theory, points to integrated systems set in motion by God. He put in place forces and constants that we know as the laws of nature. In these laws of the universe our environment exist. I can't break them, but Jesus did.

With the forces and constants of the universe in mind, I am struck by the awesome power of Christ whose words create calm and order in a storm.

❧ Reflection

Imagine you're in a small boat with a sleeping Jesus on a tumultuous body of water. The boat begins to swamp. What would you do? Why?

_____

_____

_____

_____

_____

_____

_____

_____

_____

_____

_____

_____

_____

_____

_____

_____

_____

_____

_____

_____

Weeds

"No," he answered, "because while you are pulling up the weeds, you may root up the wheat with them. Let both grow together until the harvest."

MATTHEW 13:29

Desmond Tutu once wrote, "We live in a moral universe." He's right, you know. We do live in a place of good and evil. But his observation is not simply recognition of reality. He adds, "There is no way that evil and injustice and oppression and lies can have the last word." He is very right. And that means our sustainability efforts are not in vain. Our attention to what makes the world good will win out. That is God's promise to us.

In his parable of the weeds among the wheat, Jesus lights a way ahead. It is a path filled with wisdom and patience. The sustainability movement must balance wisdom and patience in every corrective act. We cannot in essence save the environment in ways that destroy the wheat in order to remove the weeds. The world is full of evil and destruction. In order for our sustaining work to be good, our acts cannot produce evil as a by-product. For instance, if our work to save the environment burdens and oppress the poor, how can we claim it to be good? An example of this is ethanol-based fuel. The U.S. government rigidly mandates a percentage of corn production to be turned into ethanol. Doing so, in turn, increases the price of food, especially in times of drought. Thus, we burden the poor. Somehow in pursuit of a worthy ideal, we've created evil and oppression.

When we hold the wisdom and patience taught by Jesus in his parable of weeds among wheat, we keep a keen eye on not just sustainability but also moral good. In doing so, we will find ways to sustain and strengthen creation and be a force for God's goodness.

☙ Reflection

Jesus teaches us the critical importance of caring for the poor. How can you balance care for the environment and care for the poor?

_____

_____

_____

_____

_____

_____

_____

_____

_____

_____

_____

_____

_____

_____

_____

_____

_____

_____

_____

_____

_____

Seed

Jesus said, "Other seed fell into good soil and brought forth grain, growing up and increasing and yielding thirty and sixty and a hundredfold."

MARK 4:8

Like many good suburbanites, I spend many a fall Saturday or Sunday planting grass seed. While most of my lawn care activities produce little results, my sowing effort, have not been in vain—I grew lots of grass, but it just didn't last.

Moreover, despite my best efforts when sowing grass seed, seed landed everywhere: in the flower beds, on the driveway, on flagstone paths, and in the good soil. But there was one time I got it right. I took advantage of a late October warm spell to plant grass seed. When it sprouted right before Halloween, the seed produced rich, green grass, packed tightly together. What a difference planting in good soil makes.

When Jesus spoke about planting seed, I imagine him in faded blue jeans, wearing a soiled t-shirt and donning a worn high school baseball cap. He would be speaking to the guys in the neighborhood about his successes and failures tending his lawn. And Jesus had the best lawn in the neighborhood because he would always plant in good soil.

That's the heart of the story. Good soil yields rich plantings. At the heart of all we do, in sustainability or relationships with family, good soil produces a wealth of goodness and bounty.

ᘒ **Action**

In caring for the plants in your life and the relationships you cultivate, what can you do to create good soil? Create a list of five steps you can take to create good soil in all aspects of your life.

_____

_____

_____

_____

_____

_____

_____

_____

_____

_____

_____

_____

_____

_____

_____

_____

_____

_____

_____

_____

_____

_____

CHAPTER FIVE

The Vision of Restoration

And for all this, nature is never spent;
There lives the dearest freshness deep down things.

GERARD MANLEY HOPKINS

Local Farms

ROMANS 8:22

Have you heard the haunting night call of a great horned owl? Watched an Atlantic pumpkin leaf unfold? Witnessed the silent suffering of a dog giving birth? See a stag with four pointed antlers prance with pride? These days not many of us have. If we are truly steward creation; yet never glimpse its wonders or never hear its lonely song, then who are we?

Maybe we've become absentee landlords. We take from the land a fee, a price, the yielding of its labor. For most of us, we do this with little thought or care of our tenants. We dart into the grocery store or market and grab our sustenance with a swipe of plastic; even our payment has lost touch with the earth, no longer mined from the ground. If we're not absent, we seldom visit, like a distant uncle swooping in for the big party.

There is, however, another way to interact with the earth, based on Christ's vision. As Paul writes to the Romans, "The whole of creation has been groaning." It groaned for Christ's birth, his life among not just us but creation, too, and his saving death on the cross. Paul points us to a vision of totality. He means for us to understand that Jesus did not simply save humans but the world. This means the world must have needed setting free. How was and is the world captive? It was and is captive to human sin, suffering and destruction. Paul had hoped for the kingdom of heaven to reign soon after Christ's death, but we still wait for the coronation of Christ on earth. In the meantime, many carelessly consume food and creation waits.

While we expediently pour pesticides on the land, creation groans. While we alter and manipulate creation, looking only to the present, creation longs for another, saving vision.

Christ's vision is peace that comes from harmony, like the strum of a finely tuned guitar. He teaches, through his parables, the importance of tending and caring of the land and animals. When we follow his teachings, we yield a greater crop, a moral and ethical one, not just a bushel or barrel. Our purchase of food is not merely transactional; rather it is relational, informed with ethics and morality. We are in relationship with our farmers, the produce and the earth. Relationship demands presence, not absenteeism. And relationship at its best calls us to be in peace with the earth.

ᘒ Action
Research local community-supported agriculture programs (CSA). Consider purchasing a share for the next harvest season. Or for the next year, commit to buying food regularly from a farmer's market.

Peace

The nursing child shall play over the hole of the asp,
and the weaned child shall put its hand on the adder's den.

ISAIAH 11:8

While on vacation last summer, I went fly fishing on the Davidson River in the Pisgah National Forest near Brevard, North Carolina. The day was warm and beautiful, and the water was cool: perfect for fishing but not necessarily catching fish. I eased into the river, careful not to disturb too much silt and sand. I began to cast. Under a sun-dappled canopy, the rhythmic arc of the line and the placing of the fly freed my spirit from all other thought. I was at peace. I lost my sense of self and time, which is both comforting and disconcerting.

Near the end of the day, I moved down river, hiking from the road to the river through thick brush via a slit of a path. The spot was a great place to cast but was devoid of fish. Suddenly, I spotted a small timber rattlesnake essing across the river to a bush five feet from me. I looked at my sandaled feet. My disconcerting feelings grew to an awareness of my vulnerability. With no anti-venom at hand, I hiked back, with careful steps, to the car. Even with only two reported cases of snake bites in the Pisgah forest in recent years, I could no longer let go of my surroundings and be free-spirited.

The prophet Isaiah points to the sense of peace that is so fulfilling and allows our spirits to be free from the confines and constrictions of our time-bound world. It is what I experienced in the river until the snake swam by. It is not limited to fly fishing, but occurs with any earth-soul connected activity. Play is an activity that often is earth-soul connected and thus spirit-freeing.

When Isaiah envisions the infant and child playing about poisonous snake dens, we immediately sense the danger that the child doesn't. His image of playing over snake dens with no concern for danger powerfully points to a vision of the world at peace, both earth and souls. Who among us wouldn't want to inhabit such a world?

ℰ Reflection

What animals are you afraid of? Why? How different would the world be for you, if you weren't afraid of those creatures? What kind of world would that be? Why?

_____

_____

_____

_____

_____

_____

_____

_____

_____

_____

_____

_____

_____

_____

_____

_____

_____

_____

Cats and Dogs

The wolf and the lamb shall feed together,
the lion shall eat straw like the ox.

ISAIAH 65:25A

Desire and fear. Are these not the two strongest of emotions? Isaiah points us to a time when odd things will happen, such as a wolf and lamb eating together. These images foreshadow the time when desire and fear are no more.

How much of the resistance to sustainability is caught up in the desire to have more and the fear that we won't have enough? A lot. Advertisers know this. They create lovely photos of products, and beautiful images of models with handsome features pique our urges to have more. They write words that create tension and doubt to unsettle our psyche, pushing us to buy perceived protections. Advertisements enrich our feelings. It is not necessarily a bad thing. When viewing such ads, the challenge is to remember that desire and fear don't sustain us, peace and joy do.

First my family got Gracie, a sweet housecat. Then we brought home Libby, our beautiful golden retriever. When they met, it didn't go well. Gracie was so afraid, hiding in dusty corners, far under the beds. Libby simply wanted to chase Gracie. Fortunately, big dogs are slow out of the gate and cats are fast, but for a long time the house smelled of the fear of being chased and the walls dripped with the desire of chasing. Then peace came.

With training and familiarity, feline and canine became housemates. They now eat side by side, like Isaiah's wolf and lamb.

What caused the change? Maybe it's the loving hand and watchful eye of the masters of the house. Maybe it's simply the way creatures are meant to be. When we are no longer ruled by the emotions of fear and desire, the world is at peace and joy rules the creation. And we can truly unearth our sustainable souls and live in a new reality.

ℰ Action
Sit quietly for five, ten, or fifteen minutes and think about and meditate on the word, peace. Write about it.

_____

_____

_____

_____

_____

_____

_____

_____

_____

_____

_____

_____

_____

_____

_____

_____

_____

_____

A New Earth

Then I saw a new heaven and a new earth; for the first heaven and the first earth had passed away, and the sea was no more.

REVELATION 21:1

There are numerous interpretations of the Revelation of John. Regardless of how one interprets the last book of the Bible, there is no denying the power of the words contained in it. These words, from the second to last chapter, point to an awesome vision: One day there will be both a new heaven and a new earth. What does this mean? What will be new?

For one, evil will be gone and God's values will prevail, not just in heaven but on earth, not just in the future but now. This is the promise of Revelation, and it is increasing every day. Scholar and professor Stephen Cook writes, "God's new creation is irrupting into the world and increasingly demanding that human lifestyle accord with it. The book calls readers to embrace this surging new creation and its associated values, which effectively counter those of current, God-ignoring existence." We can take hope not only that the ills of the world will be righted in the future but also that God's values are being worked out now. The new earth is coming into existence now. God is calling to us now, like the early morning chittering of sparrows and the soft coos of the morning dove gently but unceasingly inviting us into a new day.

We long for days on end when our footprints in the soil, instead of being harsh stomps of destructive use and scrapings of indiscriminate power, will represent peace and joy. And yet we can see hope realized in earthly places where we have fashioned gentle footprints upon verdant fields. And yet for much of the earth, the twisting of resources lies just beyond the next hill.

ℬ **Action**

Today, pray for God's new earth to become reality. Look for where evidence of that reality is already in existence. Write about your observations.

_____

_____

_____

_____

_____

_____

_____

_____

_____

_____

_____

_____

_____

_____

_____

_____

_____

_____

_____

_____

_____

God's Joy

For you shall go out in joy, and be led back in peace;
the mountains and the hills before you shall burst into song,
and all the trees of the field shall clap their hands.

Isaiah 55:12

Imagine rising from bed each day with this verse from Isaiah before us. How wonderful each day would be! This verse draws me to memory from my late teens. It's spring, May in New England. Thick, vibrant grass covers a wide field. Its morning dew soaks my shoes. The sun rises before me with a friendly warmth on my face. It's warm, but not hot. The earth buzzes with activity. It's going to be a joyful day.

I imagine that in heaven there will be perpetual mornings like this. And yet God calls to us, even now, through creation, saying we can have heavenly mornings on earth. Maybe not on days when heavy winds bring blinding rains, nor when lightning crackles and thunder peals, neither when the sun blisters with a fiery heat on the land. Even so, most days, when God's gentleness pours forth like the love a parent has for a smiling child running into his or her arms, we walk upon a heavenly world.

When we earnestly care for the world around us, the hills sing and the trees clap. God doesn't expect perfection, as if we sail through our lives never marking the soil with work boots. God does expect us to want to live in joy with all of creation and rewards us with evenings of peaceful returns home. What could be a better way to live, "on earth as in heaven"?

⅓ **Reflection**

Think of a memory of a brilliant morning, a splendid midday, or a peaceful evening. Write about it to a friend or a family member. Explain how you felt and why.

_____

_____

_____

_____

_____

_____

_____

_____

_____

_____

_____

_____

_____

_____

_____

_____

_____

_____

_____

_____

_____

_____

_____

_____

_____

Water, Fruit and Leaves

Then the angel showed me the river of the water of life, bright as crystal, flowing from the throne of God and of the Lamb through the middle of the street of the city. On either side of the river is the tree of life, with its twelve kinds of fruit, producing its fruit each month; and the leaves of the tree are for the healing of the nations.

REVELATION 22:1–2

What is most remarkable about the ending of the Bible is that it doesn't end with humanity as its sole focus. Of course, it's about God and Christ's actions, but the tools of the restoration of humanity are the common stuff of the created world. It's the river filled with the bright, clear water of life. It is the tree of life that is on either side of the river and produces an endless supply of fruit in each month of the year. And, maybe most importantly, the leaves heal the nations.

It is worth pausing and reflecting on the options God has available to him. God's hand could touch the nations, like a mother's gentle caress. God's words could be the balm that heals them. Creation, however, is the source and instrument of God's healing. Moreover, God uses the most common and ordinary items, found everywhere in the world: water, fruit and leaves.

We should be comforted knowing that what we all are familiar with is what will ultimately be the balm for our souls, the nations, and the world. We can take heart that in spite of the chaotic and capriciousness of nature we will find great comfort in its presence when all things are made whole and when the earth is renewed.

Equally, we should see creation as privileged partners with us. No, greater than that. Creation is superior to humanity. We need creation far more than it needs us. Creation is our sustenance, hope, and balm for the sin that keeps us from joy and peace.

‽ **Reflection**

Think about the ways in which we need creation. In what ways does it heal us? How does it provide hope? How could creation be an antidote for sin?

_____

_____

_____

_____

_____

_____

_____

_____

_____

_____

_____

_____

_____

_____

_____

_____

_____

_____

CHAPTER SIX

Holy Week

Sleep sleep old Sun, thou canst not have repast
As yet, the wound thou took'st on friday last;
Sleepe then, and rest; The world may beare thy stay,
A better Sun rose before thee to day.

JOHN DONNE

Palm Branches

So they took branches of palm trees and went out to meet him, shouting, "Hosanna! Blessed is the one who comes in the name of the Lord—the King of Israel!"

JOHN 12:13

I sit listening to the trade winds rustle and rattle palm branches a few feet away. The fading December sun shimmers and shines off the swaying rich green fronds, like Christmas lights casting aglow silver strings of tinsel. What a majestic vision these five-foot palm branches would have made as they were laid down in sweeping arcs in front of Jesus. They would so completely cover the dust-caked, ecru ground that the foal would have pranced upon a carpet of solid green.

And yet, in only a few days, these fronds of celebration become vexing and uncomfortable remnants reminding passersby of what was, what is, and what they did. Discarded and tossed into corners, they become bedding for rats avoiding the searching, scorching noonday sun.

How often do we discard our resources in favor of something else? Will we advocate for the resources given us by God, or will we shrink from walking the dust-caked streets carrying a heavy, wooden cross? Streets covered with branches of palms are for those willing to sacrifice themselves and fight for something greater, just as Jesus did for all of humanity.

℘ Action

In what ways do you advocate for creation? Create a list of ways you already advocate for creation along with a list of new ways.

_____

_____

_____

_____

_____

_____

_____

_____

_____

_____

_____

_____

_____

_____

_____

_____

_____

_____

_____

_____

_____

_____

_____

_____

_____

_____

God's Keepsake

The LORD God took the man and put him in
the Garden of Eden to till it and keep it.

GENESIS 2:15

In the second creation story (Gen. 2:4–23), God creates man from the dust of the earth and then places him in the Garden of Eden "to till and keep it." Therefore, the first job, more primary than anything else we do, is to care for the earth. The job entails two parts—tilling and keeping. God calls us to work the land so that it provides sustenance for us and to preserve it. The tasks are not an either or, or a one and not the other. The acts are equally important. They are a both/and.

First, till. The word is an agrarian term that implies using resources of the earth in order to feed and provide for our communities, our families, and ourselves. Second, keep. This is a custodial term with multiple meanings. At one level it is like my daughter saying to me, "Will you keep my watch?" before she dives into a pool of water. She wants me to hold her watch so it doesn't get damaged, lost, or stolen. My daughter wants her watch back. My possession of it, my keeping, is only temporary. When God places man in the Garden, it is not to till it and destroy it, or till it until it's useless or no longer capable of producing food. No. We must keep it until God wants it back or until we pass it along to the next generation.

God calls us to keep the earth for him. It is not our possession but his. We may think of the earth as God's keepsake, a special reminder of him and our special relationship with God. Like a young lover giving a pendant necklace to his lover before his ship sails, we keep the earth close to our hearts to remember always our special love, our Lord God.

⁶ **Reflection**
In what ways are you tilling the earth?
What ways are you keeping the earth?

_____

_____

_____

_____

_____

_____

_____

_____

_____

_____

_____

_____

_____

_____

_____

_____

_____

_____

_____

_____

Stones

Jesus answered, "I tell you, if these were silent,
the stones would shout out."

LUKE 19:40

When Jesus says, "The stones would shout out," he draws a stark contrast that emphasizes his point. How can his followers be silent when he approaches Jerusalem as the victorious Messiah? Jesus is, however, making a stronger, wider point, too.

Stones are creation's wise witnesses, sage sentinels of the passing ages. As such, they know more than we of the impact of Jesus' messianic arrival. They have seen the repulsive acts of the powerful wrought upon the weak, those living simply and simply living. They have watched how Roman occupiers crafted repugnant killing devices from creation, such as the cross. So the stones would shout out if Jesus' followers "were silent" because they know a new path is being laid with the Messiah's arrival. True peace instead of oppressive power.

The stones celebrate as do we. Jesus' triumphant entry into Jerusalem is a celebration not just for humanity but for all creation. The Prince of Peace has arrived. In his words about the excitement of the stones, he calls to us, living today, to be mindful of the equal value of creation. He calls to us to think about the use of creation. Are we using it for peace or not?

❧ **Reflection**

In what ways does Jesus move you to live more sustainably? How can you be like the stone and shout out in praise of Jesus, the expert gardener, the master teacher, and your savior?

_____

_____

_____

_____

_____

_____

_____

_____

_____

_____

_____

_____

_____

_____

_____

_____

_____

_____

_____

_____

_____

_____

Gethsemane

Jesus went with them to a place called Gethsemane; and he said to his disciples, "Sit here while I go over there and pray."

MATTHEW 26:36

It's late. Jesus' breath slowly rises in a silvery mist as he quietly prays on his knees. Warmth seeps from the soil, but the dew has settled so his knees become damp. In the quiet, small creatures scamper in search of a morsel. Moonlight filters through the twisting olive tree branches and the new leaves just unfolded. Tiny, white olive blossoms shimmer in the ethereal glow, like small lanterns lighting a garden path. In this hour of darkness the world is seemingly at peace.

Jesus draws into the quiet fold of nature to connect with his father, our heavenly Father. This isn't the first time he has done this, but it's the most important one. Jesus finds solace in nature in order to steady himself for the coming chaos of Good Friday. When others are overcome with sleep, Jesus keeps slumber at bay. Or maybe he couldn't sleep, knowing his enemies are drawing near and evil is apace. Regardless, at Gethsemane, among the olive trees unfolding with flowers soon to bear fruit, Jesus prays.

For me, compared to the quiet but protected place of a church, praying outside brings with it a deep sense of vulnerability and closeness. I'm not alone, as I can be in a church sanctuary on a quiet afternoon or late night. Outdoors at night, I'm surrounded by the created world. My quiet prayers remain close. They don't rise into the rafters or toward the vaulted ceiling high above. They remain by my side. In doing so, God must draw near to hear them, like a friend whose arm is draped over another in comfort and care. To pray outside is to call on God to draw near. That is why Jesus seeks out the garden swirling with the aroma of spring and lit by the soft tones of moonlight.

❧ Action
Pray outside tonight. Find a quiet place to kneel down close to the ground and allow God to draw near.

_____

_____

_____

_____

_____

_____

_____

_____

_____

_____

_____

_____

_____

_____

_____

_____

_____

_____

_____

_____

_____

Darkness

From noon on, darkness came over the whole land
until three in the afternoon.

MATTHEW 27:45

As Jesus hung on the cross that Good Friday, more than humanity was involved. Matthew writes that "darkness came over the whole land." The image cast in my mind includes thick dark clouds, like those of a squall line, only greater. A squall lasts only a short time; it moves quickly. Matthew tells us that darkness shadowed the earth for three hours. I imagine the clouds filtering in, bringing the heaviness of humidity and forewarning of a large, blustery storm. Jesus' suffering is felt by creation. It points to his greatness and the weight of human sin upon creation.

What have we done that creation would darken at Jesus' suffering and death? Creation blots out the sun while the Son of God suffers and dies. Divine judgment of humanity's sin occurs on the cross, and darkened creation, like a witness pointing at the accused, declares us guilty. Jesus pays for our sins, the greatest of which is the ease with which we slide into God's seat and announce our right to clutch the mantle of the most high.

Although Christ has paid our debt and satisfied the necessary penalty for humanity's sin once and for all, we may succumb to the same sinful temptations that all humans encounter. Not least of the temptations is our mishandling of the good earth. Yes, the trajectory of humanity is one of learned recognition of the misuse of power, but the temptation to avail ourselves of creation's fruit thoughtlessly still vexes the human soul. Creation still darkens. In doing so, it reminds us of the cross and our need of a savior—our need for Christ.

ଋ **Reflection**

Where do you see darkness in creation these days?

_____

_____

_____

_____

_____

_____

_____

_____

_____

_____

_____

_____

_____

_____

_____

_____

_____

_____

_____

_____

_____

_____

_____

_____

_____

_____

_____

Silence

*When Jesus had received the wine, he said, "It is finished."
Then he bowed his head and gave up his spirit.*

JOHN 19:30

While I was in seminary, I lived inside the D.C. beltway. While Alexandria, Virginia, is a beautiful city with many pleasant tree-lined streets and lots of green spaces, it is surrounded by highways. A constant din of tires on asphalt reverberates through the air. It's difficult to find silence in the city, and until I lived there, I hadn't realized how much I need quiet time and space.

I longed to silence. So on a cool, early spring day, some buddies joined me on a trip down past St. Mary's City, Maryland, to Point Lookout. There, I found the silence my soul needed. When we stepped from the car, my shoes crunched on the gravel. It was the only audible noise. Immediately, my soul freshened. As we walked the paths and along the water's edge, I rediscovered my inner calmness. The silence filled my soul.

However, not all silence is good. It filled the troubling hours between Jesus' death on the cross and his triumphal rising again from the tomb. I imagine the silence of those days rent the souls of Jesus' followers. His voice was no longer present. He was gone. What was there to say? Nothing. Silence surrounded their thoughts and mental images replaying his tragic end.

When creation is silent, like those hours between his death and rising, it's not idle. Nor does this kind of silence mean absence. Silence may mean the world at rest, like the pause between heartbeats. And so silence is useful, not only in filling our souls with restorative energy, but also in making us to realize what we don't yet have. Christ's return is yet to be, and in the silence of creation we can hear our souls' longing for him to dwell with us yet again.

෨ **Action**

Find a secluded space and spend twenty minutes, forty minutes, or an hour in silence. Notice what difficulties arise in your thoughts. Listen carefully for the noises of creation. What sounds do you hear that when you're free to speak you don't notice?

_____

_____

_____

_____

_____

_____

_____

_____

_____

_____

_____

_____

_____

_____

_____

_____

_____

_____

_____

_____

_____

Easter

Jesus said to them, "Cast the net to the right side of the boat, and you will find some." So they cast it, and now they were not able to haul it in because there were so many fish.

JOHN 21:6

When I was about fourteen years old, I fished as often as I could. One day in early spring, I stood on a bowed trunk of a tree arching out away from the shore, with my line in the cold water of a clear New Hampshire lake. The water was just a foot deep. The bottom was a mix of ruddy sand, mud, and smooth, oval stones and rocks. Soon I hooked a fish and reeled it in. It was a beautiful, six-inch yellow perch. Its green, yellow, and red skin shimmered in the warm sunshine. Unfortunately, it had swallowed my hook. Patiently, but quickly, I worked gently to get the hook out.

Movement in the water below my feet caught my eye. I looked down. Every inch of water was filled with yellow perch. The hundreds of fish that had gathered below the tree I was on mesmerized me. I stole a glance at the fish in my hand. I thought if I could only free the hook, I could hook another fish in a snap. But freeing the fish took an extra minute. When I looked down at the water again, the school had left. I released my catch and it spirited away. I continued to fish, but my luck was gone. I didn't reel in another fish that afternoon.

Fishing is capricious. For a time I can hook fish after fish, and then, nothing. On more than one occasion, I've fished for hours on end and come away empty-handed, just like the disciples on that night on the Sea of Galilee after Jesus' death. I also know the onset of breathless amazement when fish seemingly catch themselves, as the disciples felt when the risen Christ directed them to lay their nets in the water one last time.

We live in a remarkably bountiful world that teems with life. The resurrection calls us to live gently and peaceably with ourselves, our neighbors, and all the rest of creation.

৪৩ Action

Take time this day to be in God's creation. Go for a walk or stand quietly and observe the world. Let your soul resonate with the created world and with God. Stay in that mystical space until you no longer know which string plays and which resonates. Give thanks for your soul, for creation, and for God. Write about your experience so you can return to it in the future.

_____

_____

_____

_____

_____

_____

_____

_____

_____

_____

_____

_____

_____

_____

_____

_____

Bibliography

Achtemeier, Paul J., ed. *The HarperCollins Bible Dictionary*. Rev. ed. New York: HarperCollins Publishers, 1996.

Bly, Robert, ed. *The Soul Is Here For Its Own Joy: Sacred Poems from Many Cultures*. Hopewell, N.J.: Ecco, 1995.

Bouma-Prediger, Steven. *For the Beauty of the Earth: A Christian Vision for Creation Care*. Grand Rapids, Mich.: Baker Academic, 2007.

Cook, Stephen L. *The Apocalyptic Literature*. Nashville, Tennessee: Abingdon, 2003.

Davis, Ellen F. *Getting Involved with God: Rediscovering the Old Testament*. New York: Rowman & Littlefield, 2001.

Donne, *John Poems and Prose (Everyman's Library Pocket Poets)*. New York: Alfred A. Knopf, 1995.

Durling, Robert M., ed. & trans. *The Divine Comedy of Dante Alighieri, Volume 1, Inferno*. New York: Oxford University Press, 1996.

Environmental Protection Agency, "Definitions of Sustainability" (Region 10: The Pacific Northwest, EPA, 2014), http://yosemite.epa.gov/r10/oi.nsf/2eae469b86eab19f88256fc40077b286/7dc483330319d2d888256fc4007842da!OpenDocument. Accessed March 6, 2014.

Henderson, Tom. "Sound Wave and Music, Lesson 5, Resonance" (Glenview, Ill.: Physics in the Classroom, 2014). http://www.physicsclassroom.com/class/sound/Lesson-5/Resonance. Accessed March 15, 2014.

Tickle, Phyllis. *The Great Emergence: How Christianity Is Changing and Why*. Grand Rapids, Mich.: Baker, 2008.

Tutu, Desmond. *God Has a Dream: A Vision of Hope for Our Time*. New York: Doubleday, 2004.

Wirzba, Norman, ed. *The Art of the Commonplace: The Agrarian Essays of Wendell Berry*. Berkeley: Counterpoint, 2002.

Index of Biblical References